RANDY
NEWMAN
ANTHOLOGY

MW01040212

Project Manager: Sy Feldman
Arrangements Supervised and Edited by Michael Roth
Management: Cathy Kerr
1250 6th Street, Suite 401
Santa Monica, CA 90401
Cover Photo: Pamela Springsteen © 1996 Warner Bros. Records/Reprise Records
Art Layout: Odalis Soto

Look for Rhino Records' GUILTY: 30 YEARS OF RANDY NEWMAN
4-CD box, the definitive career retrospective spanning Newman's 30-year career.

Editor's Note:

In putting together this anthology, much effort has been aimed towards making the *Randy Newman Anthology* a unique collection that celebrates one of the most distinctive voices in American songwriting. It is the first publication to include previously unavailable Newman classics such as "Davy the Fat Boy," "Political Science," "Burn On," and "Real Emotional Girl," and several songs from his recent musical version of *Faust,* including "Gainesville" and "Feels Like Home."

Most important, in editing this anthology I have tried to write piano arrangements that are in most cases very close to what Randy himself plays, a unique characteristic for a pop music collection, but a useful one given the distinctive style that Randy brings to the instrument. These arrangements were assembled using Randy's own notes and orchestrations, transcribing performances from various recordings and concerts, and my own time spent watching Randy play these songs over the years and trying to match his style. It should be added that since some of these songs are over 20 years old, Randy's way of performing them has evolved some. To that point, it's worth mentioning that Randy's style allows for a good amount of improvisation and it wouldn't be quite right to treat either the piano part or the notated vocal line as holy writ—guidelines would be more like it. I've kept that in mind while preparing these arrangements, as well as taking into account his orchestral style: in some cases, I've prepared a piano part that might, for example, have a first verse that is what Randy plays on the piano and a second that is essentially an orchestral reduction. Each song is arranged in Randy's key.

A few specific musical points: Randy is a born shuffler, or as he has said, he even feels clock ticks as triplets. There are different ways to notate this style of playing, and I have used several, including putting the song in 12/8 or keeping the song in 4/4 and writing the indication, ♫=♩ ♪. My advice in general is to feel the triplets a bit lazily, don't rush from one to the next, and feel the motion with a bit of weight—don't separate from one eighth to the next, as you might, for example, in a musical theatre song.

In his straight-eighth rock-and-roll songs, Randy more often than not will play a left-hand accent on the end of four, the last eighth note of the measure. Play a good solid accent on this note, and keep your hand down through the downbeat—keep the sound ringing.

Finally, and most important, don't rush, or to paraphrase Scott Joplin, it is never right to play Newman's songs fast. This is a deceptively simple instruction, but one of the most rewarding elements of playing his music is to discover how really musical and fun it is to play when you take your time.

Thanks to Bill Galliford, Ethan Neuburg and David Pugh for their initial work on the transcriptions, and to Mr. Newman for access to his archives. I've been privileged to learn to play his songs by working with him, and it is at last a pleasure to bring these arrangements to publication.

Michael Roth 8/98

RANDY NEWMAN

Dancing bears and rednecks. Good old boys and little criminals. Miscreants, saints, lovers and loonies. The music of Randy Newman has always been a richly populated world of strange and fascinating characters, situations both touching and troubling and moments of poignant and particular truth.

For over two decades, and over the course of ten ground-breaking albums, Randy Newman's music has always had a story to tell. Now, with the completion of *Faust*, his full-length musical version of one of western literature's most enduring tales, Randy Newman tells a story for the ages.

Randy Newman was born in Los Angeles to a prestigious musical family, which includes his uncles Alfred and Lionel. A musical composition student at UCLA, his first single, "Golden Gridiron Boy," produced by Pat Boone, was released in 1961. A year later Newman joined Metric Music as a staff writer and went on to pen a number of chart singles for such artists as The Fleetwoods, Gene McDaniels, Jerry Butler, Cilla Black, Alan Price, Gene Pitney, Judy Collins, Manfred Mann, Frankie Laine, Jackie DeShannon, The Walker Brothers, The Nashville Teens and others.

His eponymously titled debut vocal album was released in 1968 and contained such Newman classics as "The Beehive State," "Love Story" and "So Long Dad." In 1969, he received his first Grammy nomination for Best Arrangement Accompanying a Vocalist with Peggy Lee's "Is That All There Is?" It was followed in 1970 by *Twelve Songs,* which included "Mama Told Me (Not To Come)," later a number one hit for Three Dog Night. *Randy Newman Live,* recorded at New York's Bitter End, was released in 1971 followed by *Sail Away* (1972), highlighting the much-covered title track.

The late seventies saw the release of three quintessentially Newmanesque albums, *Good Ol' Boys* (1974), *Little Criminals* (1978), featuring the million-selling hit "Short People," and *Born Again* (1979). The early eighties marked Newman's entry into film scoring, beginning with the 1982 soundtrack to Milos Forman's *Ragtime,* a Grammy-nominee, highlighting the Oscar-nominated song "One More Hour." Nineteen eighty-three saw the release of *Trouble In Paradise* which contained the hit "I Love L.A." and was followed by the acclaimed soundtrack recording for *The Natural,* a Grammy winner for the year.

His film work continued, including songs for *The Three Amigos* in 1986, which was also Newman's first screenplay credit, in collaboration with Steve Martin and Lorne Michaels. In 1988, he released the quasi-autobiographical and critically acclaimed *Land Of Dreams* album, followed by a spate of soundtracks including the scores to *Avalon* and *Awakenings,* both Grammy nominees, as was "I Love To See You Smile" from the score to the film *Parenthood.* His more recent film scores include *The Paper, Maverick, James And The Giant Peach* and *Toy Story,* for which he received two Oscar nominations, a Golden Globe nomination and received the award from the Chicago Film Critics for Best Original Score. His latest film *Michael* from Nora Ephron starred John Travolta and was one of the holiday's major box office hits.

In between albums and film scores, Newman continued work on the music and book to *Faust,* a new American musical. Album sessions originally began in 1993 and carried over two years, in and around the artist's increasingly busy schedule. Featuring almost twenty new Newman originals, *Faust* is both a major stage production and a star-studded album on Reprise Records, highlighting performances by James Taylor, Don Henley, Elton John, Linda Ronstadt, Bonnie Raitt and Newman himself. It is also a giant step in the creative evolution of a master musical storyteller. The show premiered to critical acclaim at the La Jolla Playhouse in September of 1995. It was lauded by critics as "witty and superb," "a ferocious musical valentine" and "the next bright hope of Broadway." It was re-staged at Chicago's prestigious Goodman Theatre in the fall of 1996, becoming one of the most successful productions ever at The Goodman, and was named one of the top 10 theatrical events of 1996 by *Time* magazine.

CONTENTS

BALTIMORE

Words and Music by
RANDY NEWMAN

Moderately, steady beat ♩ = 100

Verse 1:

1. Beat - up lit - tle sea - gull, on a mar - ble

stair,___ tryin' to find the o - cean,

Baltimore - 8 - 1
PF9808

6

look-in' ev - 'ry - where._

Hard times in the cit - y, in a hard town_ by the sea.

Ain't no-where to run to.__ There ain't noth-in' here. for free.

Hook-er on the cor - ner,

8

Baltimore - 8 - 4
PF9808

Verse 2:

2. Get my sis - ter San - dy and my lit - tle bro - ther Ray.

Buy a big old wa - gon to haul us all___ a - way.

Live out in the coun - try

12

Baltimore - 8 - 8
PF9808

BLEEDING ALL OVER THE PLACE
from Randy Newman's FAUST

Words and Music by
RANDY NEWMAN

Verse (ad lib./blues style):

Why don't you love me like you used to do?_____

Are you tryin' to break my heart?

Bleeding All Over the Place - 9 - 1
PF9808

14

Lyrics:
I don't mean to be rude, but I'm in a pret-ty *bad* *mood!*

Just take a look at my face. I'm

bleed-in' all_____ o - ver the place,

bleed-in' all o - ver.

20

BURN ON

Words and Music by
RANDY NEWMAN

Moderate ♩ = 120

(with pedal)

There's a red moon ris-ing on the Cuy-a-ho-ga Riv-er, roll-ing in-to Cleve-

land to the lake. There's a red moon ris-

Burn On - 5 - 1
PF9808

There's an
Cleve-land, cit-y of light, cit-y of mag-ic.
Cleve-land, cit-y of light, you're call-ing me.
Cleve-land, e-ven now___ I can re-mem-ber, 'cause the

Burn On - 5 - 3
PF9808

26

Burn On - 5 - 5
PF9808

COWBOY

Words and Music by
RANDY NEWMAN

Maestoso

I rode a-lone. Cow-boy,___ cow-boy,___

slower, poco rubato

can't run, can't hide. It's too late to fight now,

mf

too tired___ to try.

poco rit. *a tempo*

29

Wind that once blew free now scat-ters dust to the sky. Cow-boy,___ cow-boy,___ can't run, can't hide. It's too late to fight now, too tired___ to try.

poco rit.

Cowboy - 3 - 3
PF9808

DAVY THE FAT BOY

Words and Music by
RANDY NEWMAN

Give me half a chance;

I just know you'll like my fat boy's dance.

do the fa - mous Fat___ Boy Dance for you.___

Faster (in "1")

a tempo

(with pedal)

rit.

34

Davy the Fat Boy - 5 - 5
PF9808

DIXIE FLYER

Words and Music by
RANDY NEWMAN

Dixie Flyer - 8 - 1
PF9808

Dixie Flyer - 8 - 3
PF9808

38

On the Dix - ie Fly - er,

bound for New Or - leans,___

back to her friends and her fam - 'ly in the Land of Dreams.

To Coda ⊕

(freely/semi-spoken vocal)

Her own moth-er came to meet us at the sta -

mp poco legato

Dixie Flyer - 8 - 4
PF9808

tion, her dress as black as a crow

in a coal mine.

She cried when her lit-tle girl got off the train.

Her broth-ers and her sis-ters came down from Jack-son,

40

42

Dreams.

a tempo

Repeat ad lib. and fade

Dixie Flyer - 8 - 8
PF9808

FEELS LIKE HOME
from Randy Newman's FAUST

Words and Music by
RANDY NEWMAN

44

47

Feels Like Home - 6 - 5
PF9808

48

Feels Like Home - 6 - 6
PF9808

GAINESVILLE
from Randy Newman's FAUST

Words and Music by
RANDY NEWMAN

Moderately slow ♩ = 92

p legato, sempre espressivo

(with pedal)

I was born in Gaines-ville, Flor-i-da, and my fa-ther was a tai-lor, and my moth-er ran a ca-fe near the u-ni-ver-si-ty. I've a broth-er, died a-born-ing, and an-oth-er who's a sail-or. I've a

50

52

GOD'S SONG
(THAT'S WHY I LOVE MANKIND)

Words and Music by
RANDY NEWMAN

Slow quiet blues shuffle ♩ = 69

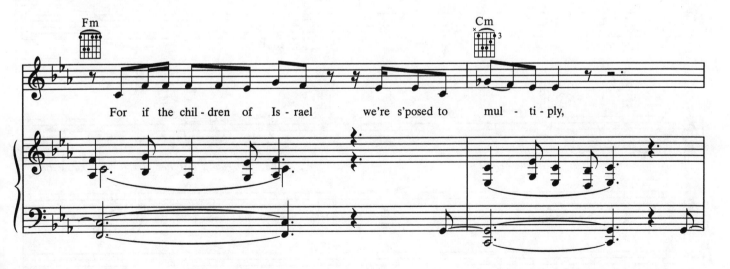

God's Song - 6 - 1
PF9808

56

58

GUILTY

Words and Music by
RANDY NEWMAN

*mm. 9 - 13: The right hand part can be played as written, or just play the left hand, ad lib.

Guilty - 4 - 3
PF9808

62

* See mm. 9 - 13.

Guilty - 4 - 4
PF9808

I LOVE L.A.

Words and Music by
RANDY NEWMAN

66

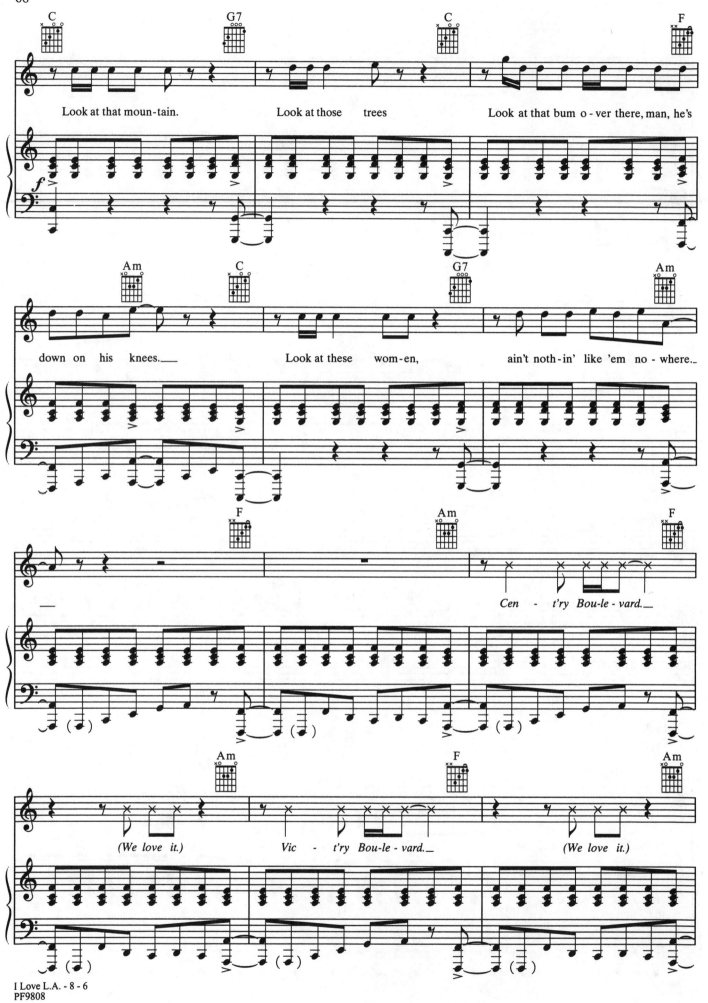

San - ta Mo - ni - ca Bou - le - vard. (We love it.) Sixth Street. (We

love it. We love it. We love it. We love it. We love___ L. A.)

(Guitar solo ad lib.)

(poco maestoso)

I Love L.A. - 8 - 7
PF9808

70

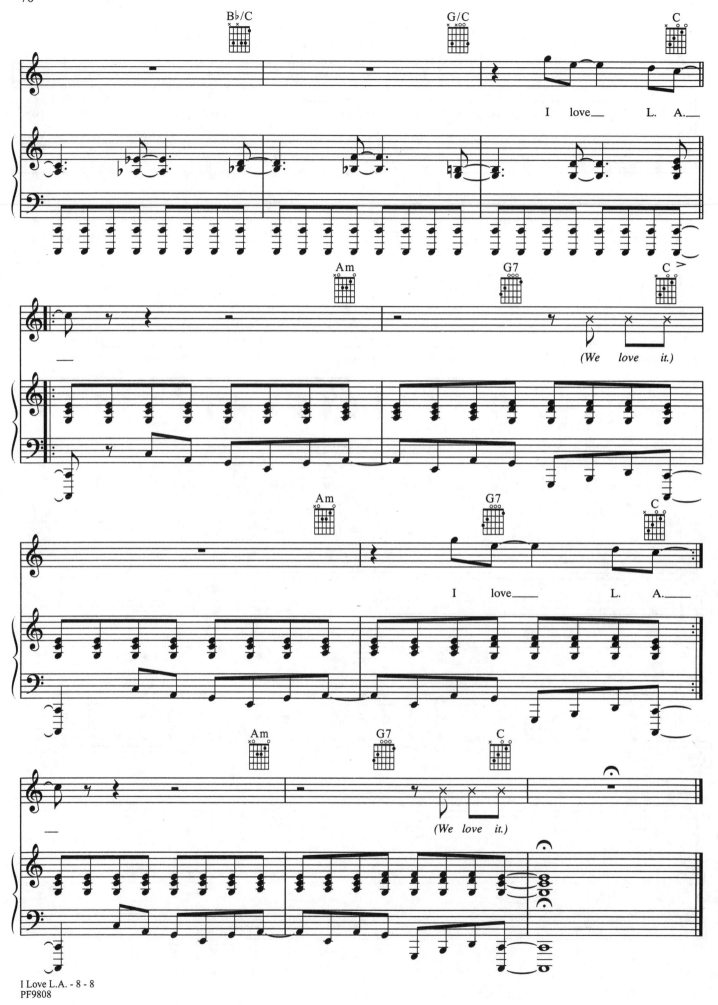

I LOVE TO SEE YOU SMILE

from the motion picture "Parenthood"

Words and Music by
RANDY NEWMAN

I Love to See You Smile - 4 - 1
PF9808

73

Verse 5:

5. In a world that's full of trou-ble,

you make it all worth-while.___ What would I do

I Love to See You Smile - 4 - 3
PF9808

74

Verse 2:
Don't want to take a trip to China.
Don't want to sail up the Nile.
Wouldn't want to get too far from where you are
'Cause I love to see you smile.

Verse 3:
(Instrumental)

Verse 4:
Like a sink without a faucet,
Like a watch without a dial,
What would I do if I didn't have you?
I love to see you smile.

I THINK IT'S GOING TO RAIN TODAY

Words and Music by
RANDY NEWMAN

76

I Think It's Going to Rain Today - 4 - 3
PF9808

Verse 3:

3. Bright be - fore___ me, the signs im - plore___ me, "Help the need - y and

show them the way." Hu - man kind - ness is

o - ver - flow - ing and I think it's go - ing___ to

rain___ to - day.

I Think It's Going to Rain Today - 4 - 4
PF9808

I WANT YOU TO HURT LIKE I DO

Words and Music by
RANDY NEWMAN

82

want_____ you to hurt like I do. Hon-est, I

do, hon-est, I do, hon-est, I do."

Verse 2:

2. If I had one wish, one dream I knew would come true,

I'd want to speak to all the peo-ple of the

I Want You to Hurt Like I Do - 6 - 4
PF9808

84

D.S. %al Coda

Coda

I Want You to Hurt Like I Do - 6 - 6
PF9808

IN GERMANY BEFORE THE WAR

Words and Music by
RANDY NEWMAN

We lie be-neath the au-tumn sky, my lit - tle gold - en girl and I. And she lies ver - y still.

IT'S MONEY THAT I LOVE

Words and Music by
RANDY NEWMAN

Verses 1 & 2:
(semi-spoken/ad lib.)

1. I don't love the moun-tains, and I don't love the sea.
2. *See additional lyrics*

It's Money That I Love - 8 - 1
PF9808

92

Bb

C

G7

(ad lib.)

To Coda ⊕

Verse 3:

3. Used___ to wor - ry   'bout the poor,___

It's Money That I Love - 8 - 4
PF9808

but I don't wor - ry an - y - more.

Used to wor - ry 'bout the black man.

Now, I don't wor - ry 'bout the black man.

Used to wor - ry 'bout the starv - ing chil - dren of In - di - a.

It's Money That I Love - 8 - 5
PF9808

93

94

It's Money That I Love - 8 - 6
PF9808

Verse 2:
They say that money
Can't buy love in this world,
But it'll get you a half-pound of cocaine
And a sixteen-year-old girl,
And a great big, long limousine
On a hot September night.
Now, that may not be love,
But it is alright.
(To Chorus 2:)

LIVING WITHOUT YOU

Words and Music by
RANDY NEWMAN

Verse 1:

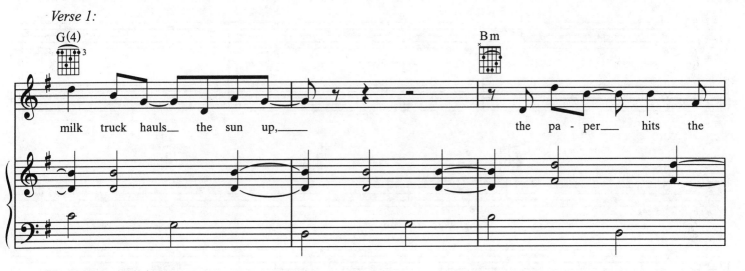

Living Without You - 4 - 1
PF9808

LONELY AT THE TOP
(a/k/a It's Lonely At the Top)

Words and Music by
RANDY NEWMAN

Lonely at the Top - 5 - 1
PF9808

104

Oh, it's lone-ly at the top.____

Lis-ten, all you fools____

Lonely at the Top - 5 - 4
PF9808

LOUISIANA 1927

Words and Music by
RANDY NEWMAN

What has hap-pened down here   is   the wind have   changed._

Louisiana 1927 - 6 - 1
PF9808

110

Louisiana 1927 - 6 - 5
PF9808

MAMA TOLD ME NOT TO COME

Words and Music by
RANDY NEWMAN

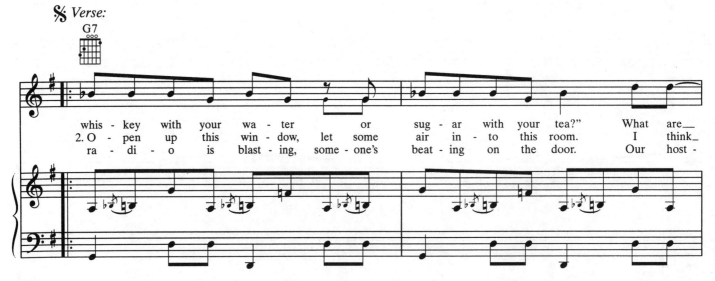

Mama Told Me Not to Come - 3 - 1
PF9808

Mama Told Me Not to Come - 3 - 3
PF9808

MARIE

Words and Music by
RANDY NEWMAN
Original String Arrangement by
Nick DeCaro

Marie - 5 - 1
PF9808

116

Marie - 5 - 2
PF9808

Some-times I'm cra - zy, but I guess you know,

and I'm weak and I'm la - zy and I hurt you so.

And I don't lis - ten to a word you say.

When you're in trou-ble, I turn a - way.

MIAMI

Words and Music by
RANDY NEWMAN

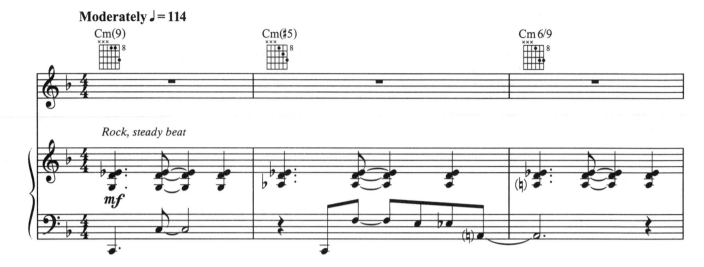

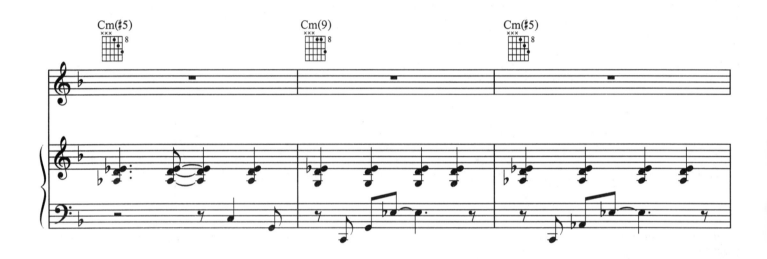

Miami - 7 - 1
PF9808

Ver - y, ver - y spe-cial. *Ver - y . . .* Gee, I love_

_ Mi - am - i! It's so nice and hot and ev - 'ry build-ing's so

pret - ty and white. And I al - ways get in - to so much trou-ble when I'm

down there. I know these

Verse 2:
There's a man over there
With the conch in his hair.
He's a very bad man.
Don't look now!
He's really very bad.
And his name's Medina
And he comes from Argentina.
See that little dog there with him?
Well, he treats it just like it was his little boy.
Oh, I love Miami!
It's so hot
And the women down here are so impure.
I love to hang around the big hotels
And sleep in the sun all day.
I know this double-jointed guy
With the circus in Saint Pete.
He's with me now.
He says hello from Fourteenth Street in . . .
(To Chorus:)

OLD MAN

Words and Music by
RANDY NEWMAN

ONE MORE HOUR
from the motion picture "Ragtime"

Words and Music by
RANDY NEWMAN

POLITICAL SCIENCE

Words and Music by
RANDY NEWMAN

Rubato, freely

No one likes us, I don't know why.___ We may not be per-fect, but heav-en knows_ we try. But all a-round_ e-ven our big friends_ put us down. Let's drop the big__ one and see what hap-pens. We

Political Science - 5 - 1
PF9808

134

REAL EMOTIONAL GIRL

Words and Music by
RANDY NEWMAN

140

Real Emotional Girl - 4 - 3
PF9808

REDNECKS

Words and Music by
RANDY NEWMAN

Freely

Last night, I saw Les-ter Mad-dox on a T V show with some

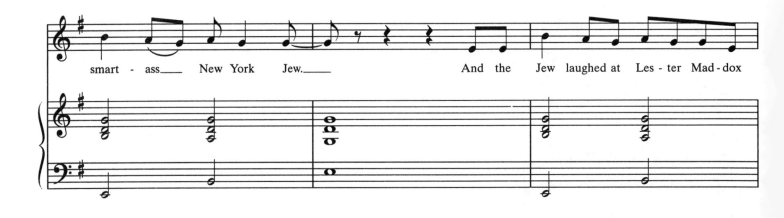

smart-ass___ New York Jew.___ And the Jew laughed at Les-ter Mad-dox

and the au-di-ence laughed at Les-ter Mad-dox too. Well, he may be a fool, but he's

Rednecks - 8 - 1
PF9808

our fool. If they think they're bet-ter than him, they're wrong.___ So, I went to the park and I took some

poco ad lib.

pa-per a-long and that's where I made this song.___ We

Moderately, strong beat ♩ = 112

G   D7   G   D7   G   D7

talk real___ fun-ny down here. We drink too___ much___ and we

poco ad lib.   *sim.*

G   D7   G   D/F♯   Em7

laugh too loud.___ We're too dumb to make it in no north-ern town and we're

146

Break:

Now, your north-ern nig-ger's a Ne-gro. You see, he's got his dig - ni - ty.

Rednecks - 8 - 5
PF9808

147

Rednecks - 8 - 6
PF9808

SAIL AWAY

Words and Music by
RANDY NEWMAN

Slowly ♩ = 69

N.C.

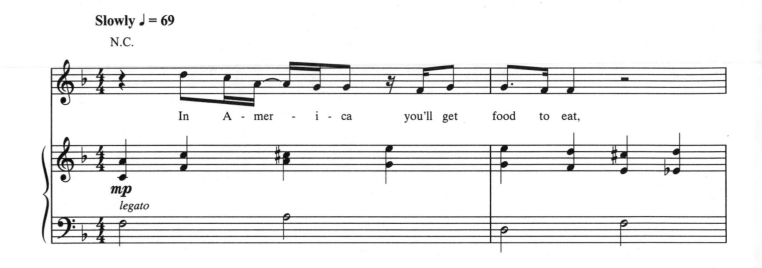

In A - mer - i - ca you'll get food to eat,

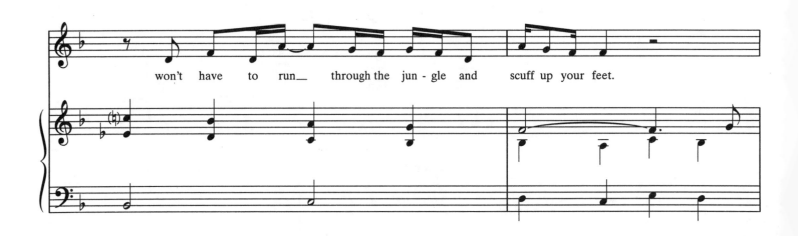

won't have to run_ through the jun - gle and scuff up your feet.

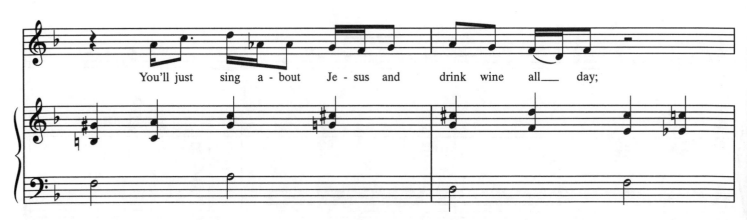

You'll just sing a - bout Je - sus and drink wine all_ day;

Sail Away - 5 - 1
PF9808

SAME GIRL

Words and Music by
RANDY NEWMAN

156

Same Girl - 4 - 2
PF9808

SANDMAN'S COMING
from Randy Newman's FAUST

Words and Music by
RANDY NEWMAN

160

Sandman's Coming - 4 - 2
PF9808

162

Sandman's Coming - 4 - 4
PF9808

SHORT PEOPLE

Words and Music by
RANDY NEWMAN

Short Peo-ple got no rea-son, short peo-ple got no rea-son,

short peo-ple got no rea-son to live._____ They got

(plus octaves ad lib.)

Short People - 5 - 1
PF9808

165

Short People - 5 - 3
PF9808

SIMON SMITH AND THE
AMAZING DANCING BEAR

Words and Music by
RANDY NEWMAN

Moderately fast with a slight swing feel ♩ = 140

170

Simon Smith and the Amazing Dancing Bear - 6 - 3
PF9808

Simon Smith and the Amazing Dancing Bear - 6 - 4
PF9808

172

’ry - where?_ It's just___ a - maz - ing how___ fair peo - ple can be._

Who___ needs mon -

Simon Smith and the Amazing Dancing Bear - 6 - 5
PF9808

Simon Smith and the Amazing Dancing Bear - 6 - 6
PF9808

SONG FOR THE DEAD

Words and Music by
RANDY NEWMAN

178

coun - try, boys.   We   won't   for - get.   We

won't   for - get.

Song for the Dead - 5 - 5
PF9808

YOU CAN LEAVE YOUR HAT ON

Words and Music by
RANDY NEWMAN

You Can Leave Your Hat On - 6 - 1
PF9808

180

You Can Leave Your Hat On - 6 - 2
PF9808

181

You Can Leave Your Hat On - 6 - 3
PF9808

YOU'VE GOT A FRIEND IN ME
from the Motion Picture "Toy Story"

Words and Music by
RANDY NEWMAN

You've got a friend in me.
You've got a friend in me.

You've got a friend in me.
You've got a friend in me.

You've Got a Friend in Me - 4 - 1
PF9808